A CATHOLIC
PRAYER BOOK

*All booklets are published thanks to the
generous support of the members of the
Catholic Truth Society*

CATHOLIC TRUTH SOCIETY
PUBLISHERS TO THE HOLY SEE

CONTENTS

Preface 5

Preparing for Prayer 6

Beginnings 7

    The Lord's Prayer 7

    Daily Dedication 8

    Glory be to the Father 8

Morning Prayer 9

    Psalm 63 10

    Psalm 149 11

    The Benedictus (Canticle of Zechariah) 12

    Intercessions 14

Prayers Throughout the Day 15

    Morning Prayer of St Francis 15

    Prayer of St Thérèse of Lisieux 15

    Prayer of Abandonment 16

    St Patrick's Breastplate 16

    Prayer for Humility 17

    Prayer of Thanksgiving 17

    Grace Before Meals 17

    Prayers to our Guardian Angel 18

    Te Deum 18

    Act of Faith, Hope and Love 20

    Come Holy Spirit 20

    Prayer for Benefactors 21

    Prayer of St Francis 21

    Prayer for Final Perseverance 22

    Prayer for Christian Unity 22

    St Patrick's Prayer 23

    Prayer of St Richard 23

    Prayer of St Ignatius Loyola 23

    Prayer to St Anthony for things that are lost 24

    An Old French Prayer for Friends 24

Prayer of Self-Dedication to Jesus Christ (Oblatio Sui) 24
Oblatio Sui (Prayer of Self-Dedication to Jesus Christ) 24
Evening Prayer of Saint Augustine 25
Prayer of Mother Teresa of Calcutta 25
Prayer of Daily Service 25
Prayer of St Teresa of Avila 26
Prayer to the Sacred Heart of Jesus 26
Preparing for Confession **27**
De Profundis 27
Act of Contrition 28, 30
I Confess 29
Prayer of Firm Purpose of Amendment 30
Prayer for Divine Mercy 32
Preparing for Mass and Holy Communion **33**
Prayer of St Ambrose 33
Prayer of St Augustine 35
Prayer of St Thomas Aquinas 36
Adoro Te Devote (Latin version) 37
Adoro Te Devote (English version) 38
Prayer of Humble Access 40
Prayer of Thomas à Kempis 40
Prayer of St Thomas More 41
Anima Christi 42
Prayer of Thanksgiving after Mass 43
Tantum Ergo 44
Prayer of Self-Dedication to Jesus Christ 45
St Teresa's Bookmark 45
Act of Petition 46
Prayer before a crucifix 46
Prayers to Our Lady **48**
Hail Mary 48
How to Say the Rosary 48

The Apostles' Creed...49
The Mysteries of the Rosary 50
Salve Regina (Hail Holy Queen) 52
The Angelus 53
Regina Caeli (by Gregory V) 55
A Child's Prayer to Mary 56
Memorare 57
Prayer for England 57
We Fly to Thy Protection 58
The Church's Oldest Prayer to Our Lady 59
Tota Pulchra Es 59
Totus Tuus 59
Maria, Mater Gratiae 59
Sancta Maria, Succurre Miseris 60
In Sickness and Death **61**
Prayer for a Happy Death 61
Prayer for the Sick 61
Prayer for the Dying 61
Prayer for the Dead 62
Prayer Immediately after Death 62
Exposition and Benediction **63**
Rite of Exposition and Benediction 63
The Divine Praises 67
Evening Prayer **68**
Psalm 110 69
Psalm 16 70
Magnificat (Canticle of Mary) 71
Intercessions 72
Night Prayer **74**
Psalm 4 75
Psalm 133 76
Nunc Dimittis (Canticle of Simeon) 77

PREFACE

'The raising of the heart and mind to God.' This traditional definition of prayer sums up what should be a regular activity for all of us. As we say at every Mass, 'It is right to give him thanks and praise.' Prayer is, first of all, acknowledging God's call and responding to Him in humility. As the *Catechism of the Catholic Church* states in a wonderful quote from St Thérèse of Lisieux: "For me, prayer is a surge of the heart; it is a simple look turned toward heaven, it is a cry of recognition and of love, embracing both trial and joy" *(CCC 2558)*.

I warmly welcome this new edition of A Catholic Prayer Book which draws on a rich treasury of prayer spanning the writings of the Old Testament and the Fathers of the Church through to some of the great saints of the Middle Ages and more recent times. I am sure that it will be a great help to all who seek to enter more deeply into the life of prayer, which is "the encounter of God's thirst with ours. God thirsts that we may thirst for him" *(CCC 2560)*.

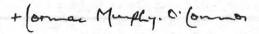

✠ **Archbishop Cormac Murphy-O'Connor**
15 August 2000, Feast of the Assumption of Our Lady

PREPARING FOR PRAYER

*From the Jesus Psalter, written by Richard Whitford, an
English Bridgettine monk, in the sixteenth century.*

Jesus, grant me grace to fix my mind on thee, especially
in time of prayer, when I directly converse with thee.

Stop the motions of my wandering head,
and the desires of my unstable heart;
suppress the power of my spiritual enemies,
who endeavour at that time to draw my mind from
heavenly thoughts, to many vain imaginations.

So shall I, with joy and gratitude,
look on thee as my deliverer from all the evils
I have escaped; and as my benefactor for all the good
I have ever received, or can hope for.
I shall see that thou art my only good,
and that all other things are but means ordained
by thee to make me fix my mind on thee,
to make me love thee more and more,
and, by loving thee, to be eternally happy.
O beloved of my soul, take up all my thoughts here,
that my eyes, abstaining from vain and hurtful sights,
may become worthy to behold thee face to face
in thy glory for ever. Amen.

BEGINNINGS

The Sign of the Cross

*Christians begin their day, their prayers, and their
activities with the Sign of the Cross. The Sign of the
Cross strengthens us in our temptations and difficulties.*

In nómine Patris, et Fílii, et Spíritus Sancti. Amen.

In the name of the Father, and of the Son, and of the Holy Spirit. Amen.

Per signum crucis de inimicis nostris líbera nos, Deus noster. In nómine Patris...

By the sign of the cross deliver us from our enemies, you who are our God. In the name...

The Lord's Prayer

*This is the prayer which Jesus taught his apostles when
they asked him to show them how to pray
(see Matthew 6:19 and Luke 11:2-4).*

Pater noster, qui es in cælis: sanctificétur nomen tuum; advéniat regnum tuum; fiat volúntas tua, sicut in cælo, et in terra.

Our Father, who art in heaven, hallowed be thy name. Thy kingdom come; Thy will be done on earth, as it is in heaven.

Panem nostrum quotidiánum da nobis hódie; et dimitte

Give us this day our daily bread, and forgive us our

nobis débita nostra, sicut et nos dimíttimus debitóribus nostris; et ne nos indúcas in tentatiónem; sed líbera nos a malo. Amen.

trespasses, as we forgive those who trespass against us, and lead us not into temptation, but deliver us from evil. Amen.

Glory be to the Father

The giving of glory and adoration to God is the basic duty of mankind, his creatures. In this form, called 'The little Doxology', it appears at the end of most psalms in the Divine Office.

Glória Patri, et Fílio, et Spirítui Sancto.

Glory be to the Father, and to the Son, and to the Holy Spirit.

Sicut erat in princípio et nunc et semper et in sǽcula sæculórum. Amen.

As it was in the beginning, is now, and ever shall be, world without end. Amen

Daily Dedication

Formerly the collect for Ember Saturday in Lent, this prayer is now used on the Thursday after Ash Wednesday.
Lord, may everything we do begin with your inspiration and continue with your help, so that all our prayers and works may begin in you and by you be happily ended. We ask this through Christ our Lord. Amen.

Morning Prayer

An order for Morning Prayer

V. O Lord open our lips
R. And we shall praise your name.
Glory be to the Father, and to the Son, and to the Holy Spirit, as it was in the beginning, is now and ever shall be, world without end. Amen. (Alleluia)

(A suitable hymn such as the following is said)
Transcendent God in whom we live,
The Resurrection and the Light,
We sing for you a morning hymn,
To end the silence of the night.

When early cock begins to crow,
And everything from sleep awakes,
New life and hope spring up again,
While out of darkness colour breaks.

Creator of all things that are,
The measure and the end of all,
Forgiving God, forget our sins,
And hear our prayer before we call.

Praise Father, Son and Holy Ghost,
Blest Trinity and source of grace,
Who call us out of nothingness,
To find in you our resting-place.

One or more of the following psalms can be said:

Psalm 63

O God, you are my God, for you I long;
for you my soul is thirsting,
My body pines for you
like a dry, weary land without water.
So I gaze on you in the sanctuary
to see your strength and your glory.

For your love is better than life,
my lips will speak your praise.
So I will bless you all my life,
in your name I will lift up my hands.
My soul shall be filled as with a banquet,
my mouth shall praise you with joy.

On my bed I remember you.
On you I muse through the night
for you have been my help;
in the shadow of your wings I rejoice.
My soul clings to you;
your right hand holds me fast.

Glory be to the Father, and to the Son, and to the Holy
Spirit, as it...

Psalm 149

Sing a new song to the Lord,
his praise in the assembly of the faithful.
Let Israel rejoice in its Maker,
let Sion's sons exult in their king.
Let them praise his name with dancing
and make music with timbrel and harp.

For the Lord takes delight in his people.
He crowns the poor with salvation.
Let the faithful rejoice in their glory,
shout for joy and take their rest.
Let the praise of God be on their lips
and a two-edged sword in their hand,
to deal out vengeance to the nations
and punishment on all the peoples;
to bind their kings in chains
and their nobles in fetters of iron;
to carry out the sentence pre-ordained:
this honour is for all his faithful.

Glory be to the Father, and to the Son, and to the Holy
Spirit, as it...

(Other psalms suitable for morning prayer include Psalms 24, 67 & 100)

Scripture Reading
Rom 13:11b, 12-13a

You know what hour it is, how it is full time now for you to wake from sleep. The night is far gone, the day is at hand. Let us cast off the works of darkness and put on the armour of light; let us conduct ourselves becomingly as in the day.

Short Responsory

R. You are the Christ, Son of the living God. Have mercy on us. *(Repeat)*
V. You are seated at the right hand of the Father.
R. You are the Christ, Son of the living God. Have mercy on us.
V. Glory be to the Father, and to the Son, and to the Holy Spirit.
R. You are the Christ, Son of the living God. Have mercy on us.

The Benedictus (Canticle of Zechariah)

Blessed be the Lord, the God of Israel!
He has visited his people and redeemed them.

He has raised up for us a mighty saviour
in the house of David his servant,
as he promised by the lips of holy men,

those who were his prophets from of old.
A saviour who would free us from our foes,
from the hands of all who hate us.
So his love for our fathers is fulfilled
and his holy covenant remembered.

He swore to Abraham our father to grant us,
that free from fear, and saved from the hands of our foes,
we might serve him in holiness and justice
all the days of our life in his presence.

As for you, little child,
you shall be called a prophet of God, the Most High.
You shall go ahead of the Lord
to prepare his ways before him.

To make known to his people their salvation
through forgiveness of all their sins,
the loving kindness of the heart of our God
who visits us like the dawn from on high.

He will give light to those in darkness,
those who dwell in the shadow of death,
and guide us into the way of peace.

Glory be to the Father, and to the Son, and to the Holy
Spirit, as it...

Intercessions

V. Let us pray to Christ our Lord, the sun who enlightens all people:

R. Lord our Saviour, give us life!

V. We thank you for the gift of this new day.

R. Lord our Saviour, give us life!

V. May your Holy Spirit guide us to do your will.

R. Lord our Saviour, give us life!

V. Help us to manifest your love to all those we meet.

R. Lord our Saviour, give us life!

V. Renew in us your gifts, may we go forth in peace.

R. Lord our Saviour, give us life!

Our Father...

Concluding Prayer

Almighty God, you have given us this day;
strengthen us with your power
and keep us from falling into sin,
so that whatever we say, or think, or do,
may be in your service and for the sake of the kingdom.
We ask this through our Lord Jesus Christ your Son,
who lives and reigns in the unity of the Holy Spirit,
ever one God, world without end. Amen.

✠ May the Lord bless us, keep us from all evil and bring us to everlasting life. Amen.

PRAYERS THROUGHOUT THE DAY

Morning Prayer of St Francis

St Francis of Assisi (1182-1226)

Lord, help me to live this day, quietly, easily;
to lean on your great strength, trustfully, restfully;
to wait for the unfolding of your will, patiently, serenely;
to meet others, peacefully, joyfully;
to face tomorrow, confidently, courageously.

Prayer of St Thérèse of Lisieux

My life is but an instant, a passing hour.
My life is but a day that escapes and flies away.
O my God! You know that to love you on earth
I only have today.

Lord, what does it matter if the future is gloomy?
To pray for tomorrow, oh no, I cannot!
Keep my heart pure, cover me with your shadow
Just for today.

O divine Pilot! whose hand guides me.
I'm soon to see you on the eternal shore.
Guide my little boat over the stormy waves in peace
Just for today.

Prayer of Abandonment
Charles de Foucauld

Father, I abandon myself into your hands;
Do with me what you will.
Whatever you may do, I thank you;
I am ready for all, I accept all.
Let only your will be done in me and in all your creatures.
I wish no more than this, O Lord.
Into your hands I commend my soul:
I offer it to you with all the love of my heart,
for I love you, Lord, and so need to give myself,
to surrender myself into your hands without reserve
and with boundless confidence, for you are my Father.

St Patrick's Breastplate

I bind unto myself today,
the power of God to hold and lead,
his eye to watch, his might to stay,
his ear to harken to my need:
the wisdom of my God to teach,
his hand to guide, his shield to ward;
the word of God to give me speech,
his heavenly host to be my guard.
Christ be with me, Christ within me,
Christ behind me, Christ before me,
Christ beside me, Christ to win me,
Christ to comfort and restore me.

Christ beneath me, Christ above me,
Christ in quiet, Christ in danger,
Christ in hearts of all that love me,
Christ in mouth of friend and stranger.

Prayer for Humility

St Alphonsus Ligouri

Most humble Jesus, give me a share of your humility.
Take from my heart everything that displeases you;
convert it totally to you,
so that I may no longer will or desire
anything other than what you will.

Prayer of Thanksgiving

We give you thanks for all your gifts,
Almighty God, living and reigning now and forever.
Amen.

Grace Before Meals

Bless us, O Lord, and these thy gifts which we are about
to receive through thy bounty.
Through Christ our Lord.
Amen.

Prayer to our Guardian Angel

Angel sent by God to guide me,
be my light and walk beside me;
be my guardian and protect me;
on the paths of life direct me.

Angel of God

Angel of God, my guardian dear,
to whom God's love commits me here,
ever this day (or night) be at my side,
to light, to guard, to rule and guide. Amen.

Te Deum

*Written at the beginning of the fifth century,
perhaps by St Nicetas of Remesiana (335-415)*

You are God; we praise you;
You are the Lord; we acclaim you;
You are the eternal Father.
All creation worships you.
To you all angels, all the powers of heaven,
Cherubim and Seraphim, sing in endless praise;
Holy, holy, holy Lord, God of power and might,
heaven and earth are full of your glory.
The glorious company of apostles praise you.
The noble fellowship of prophets praise you.
The white-robed army of martyrs praise you.
Throughout the world the holy Church acclaims you;

Father, of majesty unbounded,
your true and only Son, worthy of all worship,
and the Holy Spirit, advocate and guide.
You, Christ, are the king of glory,
the eternal Son of the Father.
When you became man to set us free
you did not spurn the Virgin's womb.
You overcame the sting of death,
and opened the kingdom of heaven to all believers.
You are seated at God's right hand in glory.
We believe that you will come, and be our judge.
Come then, Lord and help your people,
bought with the price of your own blood,
and bring us with your saints
to glory everlasting.

Save your people, Lord, and bless your inheritance.
Govern and uphold them now and always.
Day by day we bless you.
We praise your name for ever.
Keep us today, Lord, from all sin.
Have mercy on us, Lord, have mercy.
Lord, show us your love and mercy;
for we put our trust in you.
In you, Lord, is our hope;
and we shall never hope in vain.

Act of Faith, Hope and Love

My God, I believe in you,
I trust in you,
I love you above all things,
with all my heart and mind and strength.
I love you because you are supremely
good and worth loving;
and because I love you,
I am sorry with all my heart for offending you.
Lord, have mercy on me, a sinner.
Amen.

Come Holy Spirit

*The first versicle and response are taken from the alleluia
verse before the gospel of Pentecost; the second versicle
and response from the third antiphon for the Office of
Readings on Pentecost and the prayer from the votive
Mass of the Holy Spirit in the Roman Missal.*

V. Come, Holy Spirit, fill the hearts of your faithful
R. And kindle in them the fire of your love.
V. Send forth your Spirit and they shall be created
R. And you will renew the face of the earth.

Let us pray.
Lord, by the light of your Holy Spirit
you have taught the hearts of your faithful.

In that same Spirit
help us to relish what is right
and always rejoice in your consolation.
We ask this through Christ our Lord.
R. Amen.

Prayer for Benefactors

Reward those who have been good to us
for the sake of your name, O Lord
and give them eternal life. Amen.

Prayer of St Francis

St Francis of Assisi (1182-1226)

Lord make me an instrument of your peace;
where there is hatred, let me sow love;
where there is injury, pardon;
where there is discord, union;
where there is doubt, faith;
where there is despair, hope;
where there is darkness, light;
where there is sadness, joy;
O Divine Master, grant that I may not so much seek to be
consoled as to console,
to be understood as to understand, to be loved as to love.
For it is in giving that we receive.
It is in pardoning that we are pardoned,
and it is in dying that we are born to eternal life. Amen.

Prayer for Final Perseverance

St Alphonsus Ligouri

Our dear Redeemer,
relying on your promises,
because you are faithful, all-powerful and merciful,
we hope, through the merits of your Passion,
for the forgiveness of our sins,
perseverance until death in your grace;
and at length we hope, by your mercy,
to see and love you eternally in heaven.

Prayer for Christian Unity

John Henry Newman; adapted from
'Meditations and Devotions.'

O Lord Jesus Christ,
when you were about to suffer,
you prayed for your disciples to the end of time,
that they might all be one,
as you are in the Father,
and the Father in you.
Look down in pity on the many divisions
among those who profess your faith and heal the wounds
which the pride of man and the craft of Satan have
inflicted on your people.
Break down the walls of separation which divide one
party and denomination of Christians from another.
Look with compassion on the souls who have been born

in one or another of these various communions and bring them all into that one communion which you set up in the beginning: the One, Holy, Catholic and Apostolic Church.

St Patrick's Prayer

I arise today, through the power of the Trinity, through the faith in threeness, through trust in the oneness of the Maker of the earth, and the Maker of heaven.

Prayer of St Richard

St Richard of Chichester (1198-1253)

Praise be to Thee, O Lord Jesus Christ,
For all the benefits which You have given us,
For all the pains and insults which You have borne for us.
O most merciful Redeemer, Friend and Brother,
May we see You more clearly, love You more dearly,
And follow You more nearly, Day by day. Amen.

Prayer of St Ignatius Loyola

St Ignatius Loyola (1491-1556)

Teach us Good Lord, To serve You as You deserve,
To give and not to count the cost,
To fight and not to heed the wounds,
To toil and not to seek for rest,
To labour and not to ask for any reward,
Save that of knowing that we do Your will. Amen.

Prayer to St Anthony for things that are lost

O great St Anthony, who has received from God a special power to recover lost things, help me that I may find that which I am now seeking.

An Old French Prayer for Friends

Blessed Mother of those whose names you can read in my heart, watch over them with every care. Make their way easy and their labours fruitful. Dry their tears if they weep; sanctify their joys; raise their courage if they weaken; restore their hope if they lose heart, their health if they be ill, truth if they err, and repentance if they fall. Amen.

Prayer of Self-Dedication to Jesus Christ (Oblatio Sui)

Ascribed to St Ignatius of Loyola (1491-1556)

Lord Jesus Christ, take all my freedom, my memory, my understanding, and my will. All that I have and cherish you have given me. I surrender it all to be guided by your will. Your grace and your love are wealth enough for me. Give me these, Lord Jesus, and I ask for nothing more.

Oblatio Sui (Prayer of Self-Dedication to Jesus Christ)

Suscipe, Domine, universam mean libertatem. Accipe memoriam, intellectum atque voluntatem omnem. Quidquid habeo vel possideo, mihi largitus es: id tibi totum restituo, ac tuae prorsus voluntati trado gubernandum. Amorem tui solum cum gratia tua mihi dones, et dives sum satis, nec aliud quidquam ultra posco.

Evening Prayer of St Augustine

Watch, Lord, with those who wake or weep tonight. Give the angels and saints charge over those who sleep. O Lord Jesus Christ, tend Your sick ones, rest Your weary ones, bless Your dying ones, soothe the suffering ones, pity all the afflicted ones, shield the joyful ones, and all for Your love's sake. Amen.

Prayer of Mother Teresa of Calcutta

Founder of the Missionaries of Charity (1910-1997)
The fruit of Silence is Prayer.
The fruit of Prayer is Faith.
The fruit of Faith is Love.
The fruit of Love is Service.

Prayer of Daily Service

Make us worthy, Lord, to serve our fellow men throughout the world who live and die in poverty and hunger. Give them through our hands this day their daily bread, and by our understanding love, give peace and joy. Make us, Lord, worthy to serve our brothers and sisters who are scattered all over the world, who live and die alone and poor. Give them today, using our hands, their daily bread. And, using our love, give them peace and happiness. Amen.

Prayer of St Teresa of Avila

My God, dispose of me, and of all that belongs to me, according to your good pleasure. Amen.

Prayer to the Sacred Heart of Jesus

John Henry Cardinal Newman (1801-1890)

Most sacred, most loving Heart of Jesus, you are concealed in the Holy Eucharist, and you bear for us still. Now, as then, you say: "With desire I have desired." I worship you with all my best love and awe, with fervent affection, with my most subdued, most resolved will. For a while you take up your abode within me. O make my heart beat with your Heart! Purify it of all that is earthly, all that is proud and sensual, of all perversity, of all disorder. So fill it with you, that neither the events of the day, nor the circumstance of the time, may have the power to ruffle it; but that in your love and your fear, it may have peace. Amen.

Preparing for Confession

De Profundis

Psalm 130

Out of the depths I cry to you, O Lord,
Lord, hear my voice!
O let your ears be attentive
to the voice of my pleading.
If you, O Lord, should mark our guilt,
Lord, who would survive?
But with you is found forgiveness;
for this we revere you.
My soul is waiting for the Lord,
I count on his word.
My soul is longing for the Lord,
more than watchmen for daybreak.
(Let the watchman count on daybreak
and Israel on the Lord.)
Because with the Lord there is mercy
and fullness of redemption,
Israel indeed he will redeem from all its iniquity.
Glory be to the Father, and to the Son,
and to the Holy Spirit;
as it was in the beginning,

is now, and ever shall be,
world without end,
Amen.

Act of Contrition

*This prayer is taken from
the revised Rite of Penance, 1974.*

My God,
I am sorry for my sins with all my heart.
In choosing to do wrong
and failing to do good,
I have sinned against you
whom I should love above all things.
I firmly intend,
with your help,
to do penance,
to sin no more,
and to avoid whatever leads me to sin.
Our Saviour Jesus Christ suffered and died for us.
In his name, my God, have mercy.
Amen.

Confíteor

Confíteor Deo omnipoténti, beátæ Maríæ semper Vírgini, beáto Michaéli Archángelo, beáto Ioánni Baptístæ, sanctis apostólis Petro et Paulo, ómnibus Sanctis, et vobis, fratres: quia peccávi nimis cogitatióne, verbo et ópere: mea culpa, mea culpa, mea máxima culpa.

Ideo precor beátam Maríam semper Vírginem, béatum Michaélem Archángelum, beátum Ioánnem Baptístam, sanctos apóstolos Petrum et Paulum, omnes Sanctos, et vos, fratres, oráre pro me ad Dómimum, Deum nostrum.

I Confess

I confess to almighty God, to blessed Mary ever Virgin, to blessed Michael the archangel, to blessed John the Baptist, to the holy apostles Peter and Paul, and to all the saints, that I have sinned exceedingly in thought, word and deed, through my fault, through my fault, through my most grievous fault. Therefore, I beseech blessed Mary ever Virgin, blessed Michael the archangel, blessed John the Baptist, the holy apostles Peter and Paul, and all the saints, to pray for me to the Lord our God.

Act of Contrition

St John Chrysostom (adapted)

O God, loose, remit, and forgive my sins against you,
whether in word, in deed, or in thought;
and whether they are willingly or unwillingly,
knowingly or unknowingly committed, forgive them all.
For you are good and you love all human beings.
And through the prayers of your most holy Mother,
or your heavenly servants and holy spirits,
and all the Saints who have found favour with you,
enable me to receive without condemnation your holy
Body and your Precious Blood.
Let my soul and body be thus healed and my evil
imaginings be driven away,
for yours is the kingdom,
the power, and the glory: Father, Son, and Holy Spirit,
now and forever. Amen

Prayer of Firm Purpose of Amendment

Prayer of St Benedict of Nursia (480-547)

O Lord, I place myself in your hands and dedicate myself
to you. I pledge myself to do your will in all things: To
love the Lord God with all my heart, all my soul, all my
strength. Not to kill. Not to steal. Not to covet. Not to
bear false witness. To honour all persons. Not to do to
another what I would not wish done to myself. To
chastise the body. Not to seek after pleasures. To love

fasting. To relieve the poor. To clothe the naked. To visit the sick. To bury the dead. To help in trouble. To console the sorrowing. To hold myself aloof from worldly ways. To prefer nothing to the love of Christ. Not to give way to anger. Not to foster a desire for revenge. Not to entertain deceit in the heart. Not to make a false peace. Not to forsake charity. Not to swear, lest I swear falsely. To speak the truth with heart and tongue. Not to return evil for evil. To do no injury: yes, even to bear patiently any injury done to me. To love my enemies. Not to curse those who curse me, but rather to bless them. To bear persecution for justice's sake. Not to be proud. Not to be given to intoxicating drink. Not to be an over-eater. Not to be lazy. Not to be slothful. Not to be a murmurer. Not to be a detractor. To put my trust in God. To refer the good I see in myself to God. To refer any evil in myself to myself. To fear the day of judgement. To be in dread of hell. To desire eternal life with spiritual longing. To keep death before my eyes daily. To keep constant watch over my actions. To remember that God sees me everywhere. To call upon Christ for defence against evil thoughts that arise in my heart. To guard my tongue against wicked speech. To avoid much speaking. To avoid idle talk. To read only what is good to read. To look at only what is good to see. To pray often. To ask forgiveness daily for my sins, and to seek ways to amend my life. To obey my superiors in all things rightful. Not to desire to be thought holy, but to seek holiness. To fulfill the commandments of God by good works. To love chastity. To hate no one. Not to be jealous or envious of anyone. Not to love strife. Not to love pride. To honour the aged. To pray for my enemies. To make peace after a quarrel, before the setting of the sun. Never to despair of your mercy, O God of Mercy. Amen.

Prayer for Divine Mercy

From the Diary of Saint Maria Faustina of the Sisters of Our Lady of Mercy (1905-1938)

O Greatly Merciful God, Infinite Goodness, today all mankind calls out from the abyss of its misery to Your mercy - to Your compassion, O God; and it is with its mighty voice of misery that it cries out: Gracious God, do not reject the prayer of this earth's exiles! O Lord, Goodness beyond our understanding. Who are acquainted with our misery through and through, and know that by our power we cannot ascend to You, we implore You, anticipate us with Your grace and keep on increasing Your mercy in us, that we may faithfully do Your holy will all through our life and at death's hour. Let the omnipotence of Your mercy shield us from the darts of our salvation's enemies, that we may with confidence, as Your children, await Your final coming - that day known to You alone. And we expect to obtain everything promised us by Jesus in spite of all our wretchedness. For Jesus is our Hope: Through His merciful Heart as through an open gate we pass through to heaven.

PREPARING FOR MASS AND HOLY COMMUNION

Prayer of St Ambrose

Preparation for Mass; attributed to St Ambrose
(c. 339-397), bishop of Milan

Lord Jesus Christ,
I approach your banquet table in fear and trembling,
for I am a sinner and dare not rely on my own worth
but only on your goodness and mercy.
I am defiled by many sins in body and soul
and by my unguarded thoughts and words.
Gracious God of majesty and awe,
I seek your protection,
I look for your healing.
Poor troubled sinner that I am,
I appeal to you, the fountain of all mercy.
I cannot bear your judgement,
but I trust in your salvation.
Lord, I show my wounds to you
and uncover my shame before you.
I know my sins are many and great
and they fill me with fear,
but I hope in your mercies,
for they cannot be numbered.
Lord Jesus Christ, eternal king,

divine and human,
crucified for humanity,
look upon me with mercy and hear my prayer,
for I trust in you...
Have mercy on me,
full of sorrow and sin,
for the depth of your compassion never ends.
Praise to you, saving sacrifice,
offered on the wood of the cross for me and for all.
Praise to the noble and precious blood
flowing from the wounds of my crucified Lord,
Jesus Christ and washing away the sins of the
whole world.
Remember, Lord, your creatures,
whom you have redeemed with your blood.
I repent of my sins
and I long to put right what I have done.
Merciful Lord, take away all my offences and sins;
purify me in body and soul,
and make me worthy to taste the holy of holies.
May your body and blood,
which I intend to receive, although I am unworthy,
be for me the remission of my sins,
the washing away of my guilt,
the end of my evil thoughts
and the rebirth of my better instincts.

May it spur me on to works pleasing to you and be profitable to my health in body and soul and a firm defence against the wiles of my enemies.
Amen.

Prayer of St Augustine

Lord Jesus, let me know myself and know you,
And desire nothing, save only you.
Let me hate myself and love you.
Let me do everything for the sake of you.
Let me humble myself and exalt you.
Let me think of nothing except you.
Let me accept whatever happens as from you.
Let me banish self and follow you,
And ever desire to follow you.
Let me fly from myself and take refuge in you,
That I may deserve to be defended by you.
Let me fear for myself, let me fear you,
And let me be among those who are chosen by you.
Let me be willing to obey for the sake of you.
Let me cling to nothing, save only to you,
And let me be poor because of you.
Look upon me, that I may love you.
Call me, that I may see you,
And for ever enjoy you. Amen.

Prayer of St Thomas Aquinas

Preparation for Mass; attributed to St Thomas Aquinas
(c. 1225-1274)

Almighty and ever-living God,
I approach the sacrament of your only-begotten Son,
our Lord Jesus Christ.
I come sick to the doctor of life,
unclean to the fountain of mercy,
blind to the radiance of eternal light,
poor and needy to the Lord of heaven and earth.
Lord in your great generosity,
heal my sickness, wash away my defilement,
enlighten my blindness, enrich my poverty,
and clothe my nakedness.
May I receive the bread of angels,
the King of kings and Lord of lords,
with humble reverence,
with purity and faith,
with the repentance and love
and the determined purpose
that will help to bring me to salvation.
May I receive the sacrament of the Lord's
body and blood
and its reality and power.
Kind God,
may I receive the body of your only begotten Son,
our Lord Jesus Christ,

born from the womb of the Virgin Mary,
and so be received into his mystical body
and numbered among his members.
Loving Father,
as on my earthly pilgrimage
I now receive your beloved Son
under the veil of a sacrament,
may I one day see him face to face in glory,
who lives and reigns with you for ever.
Amen.

Adoro Te Devote (Latin version)

Attributed to St Thomas Aquinas (c. 1225-1274)

Adóro te devóte, latens Déitas,
Quæ sub his figúris vere látitas:
Tibi se cor meum totum súbiicit,
Quia te contémplans totum déficit.

Visus, tactus, gustus in te fállitur,
Sed audítu solo tuto créditur.
Credo, quidquid dixit Dei Fílius:
Nic hoc verbo Veritátis vérius.

In cruce latébat sola Déitas,
At hic latet simul et humánitas;
Ambo tamen credens atque cónfitens,
Peto quod petívit latro paénitens.

Plagas, sicut Thomas, non intúeor;
Deum tamen meum te confíteor.

Fac me tibi semper magis crédere,
In te spem habére, te dilígere.

O memoriále mortis Dómini!
Panis vivus, vitam præstans hómini!
Præsta meæ menti de te vívere.
Et te illi semper dulce sápere.

Pie pellicáne, Iesu Dómine,
Me immúndum munda tuo sánguine.
Cuius una stilla salvum fácere
Totum mundum quit ab omni scélere.

Iesu, quem velátum nunc aspício,
Oro fiat illud quod tam sítio;
Ut te reveláta cernens fácie,
Visu sim beátus tuæ glóriæ. Amen.

Adoro Te Devote (English version)

Attributed to St Thomas Aquinas (c. 1225-1274)

Hidden here before me, Lord, I worship you,
Hidden in these symbols, yet completely true.
Lord, my soul surrenders, I longing to obey,
And in contemplation wholly faints away.

Seeing, touching, tasting; these are all deceived;
Only through the hearing can it be believed.
Nothing is more certain; Christ has told me so;
What the Truth has uttered, I believe and know.

Only God was hidden when you came to die;
Human nature also here escapes the eye.
Both are my profession, both are my belief;
Bring me to your Kingdom like the dying thief.

I am not like Thomas, who could see and touch;
Though your wounds are hidden, I believe as much.
Let me say so boldly, meaning what I say.
Loving you and trusting, now and every day.

Record of the Passion when the Lamb was slain,
Living bread that brings us back to life again;
Feed me with your presence, make me live on you;
Let that lovely fragrance fill me through and through.

Once a nesting pelican gashed herself to blood
For the preservation of her starving brood;
Now heal me with your blood, take away my guilt;
All the world is ransomed if one drop is spilt.

Jesus, for the present seen as through a mask,
Give me what I thirst for, give me what I ask;
Let me see your glory in a blaze of light,
And instead of blindness give me, Lord, my sight.
Amen.

The Prayer of Humble Access

*The Book of Common Prayer, based on a prayer of
St Ambrose*

We do not presume to come to this your table,
O merciful Lord, trusting in our own righteousness,
but in your many and great mercies.
We are not worthy even to gather up
the crumbs under your table.

But you are the same God whose property
is always to have mercy:
grant us, therefore, gracious Lord,
so to eat the flesh of your dear Son Jesus Christ,
and to drink his blood,
that our sinful bodies may be made clean by his body,
and our souls washed through his most precious blood,
and that we may evermore dwell in him and he in us.

Prayer of Thomas à Kempis

Lord Jesus Christ,
to whom belongs all that is in heaven and earth,
I desire to consecrate myself wholly to you and be yours
for evermore.
This day I offer myself to you in singleness of heart,
to serve and obey you always,
and I offer you without ceasing a sacrifice of praise and
thanksgiving.

Receive me, O my Saviour,
in union with the holy oblation of your precious blood
which I offer to you this day,
in the presence of angels,
that this sacrifice may avail unto my salvation and that of
the whole world.

Prayer of St Thomas More

Give me, good Lord, a full faith, and fervent charity,
a love of you, good Lord,
incomparable above the love of myself;
and that I love nothing to your displeasure,
but everything in order to serve you.
Take from me, good Lord,
this lukewarm fashion, or rather,
this cold manner of meditation,
and this dullness in praying to you.
Give me warmth, delight, and life in thinking about you.
And give me your grace to long for your holy sacraments
and specially to rejoice in the presence of your blessed
body, my sweet Saviour Jesus Christ,
in the holy sacrament of the altar,
and duly to thank you for your graciousness in giving
yourself to me.

Anima Christi

*Thanksgiving after Mass; early fourteenth century,
familiar in English as the hymn
'Soul of my Saviour'.*

Anima Christi, sanctífica me.

Soul of Christ, sanctify me.

Corpus Christi, salva me.

Body of Christ, heal me.

Sanguis Christi, inébria me.

Blood of Christ, drench me.

Aqua láteris Christi, lava me.

Water from the side of Christ, wash me.

Pássio Christi, confórta me.

Passion of Christ, strengthen me.

O bone Iesu, exáudi me.

Good Jesus, hear me.

Intra tua vúlnera abscónde me.

In your wounds shelter me.

Ne permíttas me separári a te.

From turning away keep me.

Ab hoste malígno defénde me.

From the evil one protect me.

In hora mortis meæ voca me.

At the hour of my death call me.

Et iube me venire ad te, ut cum Sanctis tuis laudem te in sæcula sæculórum. Amen.

Into your presence lead me, to praise you with all your saints for ever and ever. Amen.

Prayer of Thanksgiving after Mass

Attributed to St Thomas Aquinas (c. 1225-1274)

Lord, Father, all-powerful and ever-living God.
I thank you,
for even though I am a sinner
and your unprofitable servant,
you have fed me with the precious body
and blood of your Son,
our Lord Jesus Christ, not because of my worth
but out of your kindness and your mercy.
I pray that this holy communion
may not bring me condemnation and punishment
but forgiveness and salvation.
May it be a helmet of faith
and a shield of good will.
May it purify me from evil ways
and put an end to my evil passions.
May it bring me charity and patience,
humility and obedience,
and growth in the power to do good.
May it be my strong defence
against all my enemies, visible and invisible,
and the perfect calming of all my evil impulses,
bodily and spiritual.
May it unite me more closely to you,
the one true God,

and lead me safely through death
to everlasting happiness with you.
And I pray that you will lead me, a sinner,
to the banquet where you,
with your Son and the Holy Spirit
are true and perfect light,
total fulfillment, everlasting joy,
gladness without end,
and perfect happiness to your saints.
Grant this through Christ our Lord. Amen.

Tantum Ergo

Last two verses of a hymn written about 1264
by St Thomas Aquinas (c. 1225-1274)

Therefore we, before him bending,
This great Sacrament revere;
Types and shadows have their ending.
for the newer rite is here;
Faith, our outward sense befriending,
Makes the inward vision clear.

Glory let us give, and blessing
To the Father and the Son;
Honour, might, and praise addressing,
While eternal ages run;
Ever to his love confessing,
Who, from both, with both is one. Amen.

Prayer of Self-Dedication to Jesus Christ

Thanksgiving after Mass attributed to St Ignatius Loyola
(c.1491-1556)

Lord Jesus Christ,
take my freedom,
my memory, my understanding and my will.
All that I have and cherish,
you have given me.
I surrender it all to be guided by your will.
Your grace and your love are wealth enough for me.
Give me these, Lord Jesus,
and I ask for nothing more.

St Teresa's Bookmark

St Teresa of Avila (1515-1582)

Let nothing disturb you,
Nothing frighten you.
All things are passing,
God never changes.
Patient endurance
Attains all things.
Whom God possesses
In nothing is wanting.
Alone God suffices.

Act of Petition

St Augustine of Hippo

Give me yourself,
O my God, give yourself to me.
Behold I love you,
and if my love is too weak a thing,
grant me to love you more strongly.
I cannot measure my love to know how much it falls
short of being sufficient,
but let my soul hasten to your embrace
and never be turned away until it is hidden
in the secret shelter of your presence.
This only do I know,
that it is not good for me when you are not with me,
when you are only outside me.
I want you in my very self.
All the plenty in the world
which is not my God is utter want.

Prayer before a crucifix

*This prayer of thanksgiving after Mass
is as given in the Roman Missal since 1570*

Good and gentle Jesus,
I kneel before you.
I see and ponder your five wounds.
My eyes behold what David prophesied about you;

'They have pierced my hands and feet;
they have counted all my bones.'
Engrave on me this image of yourself.
Fulfill the yearnings of my heart;
give me faith, hope and love,
repentance for my sins
and true conversion of life. Amen.

Prayers to Our Lady

Hail Mary

The first line is the Salutation of the Archangel Gabriel to the future mother of Jesus. The second and third lines are the words of Elizabeth, her cousin; the addition of the word 'Jesus' is attributed to Pope Urban IV (1261-64), while the concluding petition reached its present form in 1514.

Ave María, gratia plena, Dóminus tecum; benedícta tu in muliéribus, et benedíctus fructus ventris tui, Iesus. Sancta Maria, Mater Dei, ora pro nobis peccatoribus, nunc et in hora mortis nostrae. Amen.

Hail, Mary, full of grace, the Lord is with thee; blessed art thou among women, and blessed is the fruit of thy womb, Jesus. Holy Mary, Mother of God, pray for us sinners, now, and at the hour of our death. Amen.

How to Say the Rosary

"The Rosary is a gospel prayer. The orderly and gradual unfolding of the Rosary reflects the very way in which the Word of God, mercifully entering into human affairs, brought about redemption." (Pope Paul VI, *Marialis Cultus* (1974) n. 44)

If you have a set of Rosary beads, first kiss the crucifix, then make the sign of the cross holding the Rosary in your right hand and say:

In the name of the Father, and of the Son, and of the Holy Spirit. Amen.

Then on the first bead above the crucifix say:

The Apostles' Creed

Credo in Deum, Patrem omnipoténtem, Creatórem cæli et terræ. Et in Iesum Christum, Fílium eius únicum, Dóminum nostrum: qui concéptus est de Spíritu Sancto, natus ex María Vírgine, passus sub Póntio Piláto, crucifíxus, mórtuus, et sepúltus; descéndit ad inferos; tértia die resurréxit a mórtuis; ascéndit ad cælos; sedet ad déxteram Dei Patris omnipoténtis; inde ventúrus est iudicáre vivos et mórtuos. Credo in Spíritum Sanctum, sanctam Ecclésiam Cathólicam, Sanctórum communiónem, remissiónem peccatórum,

I believe in God, the Father almighty, creator of heaven and earth. I believe in Jesus Christ, his only Son, our Lord. He was conceived by the power of the Holy Spirit and born of the Virgin Mary. He suffered under Pontius Pilate, was crucified, died and was buried. He descended to the dead. On the third day he rose again. He ascended into heaven and is seated at the right hand of the Father. He will come again to judge the living and the dead. I believe in the Holy Spirit, the holy Catholic Church, the communion of saints,

carnis resurrectiónem,   the forgiveness of sins, the
vitam ætérnam.   resurrection of the body and
Amen.   life everlasting. Amen.

Then on each of the three following beads say the:
Hail Mary (see page 48)

*Traditionally these three Hail Marys are said for the
intentions of the Holy Father.*
On the first bead in the main part of the Rosary say:
The Lord's Prayer (see page 7)

*This is followed by ten Hail Marys on the next ten beads.
The decade is concluded with a:*
Glory be (see page 8)

*While saying these prayers we also meditate on the events
of the life of Christ and of his mother. These are called
the mysteries of the Rosary.*
*A complete Rosary consists of twenty decades, but it is
usual to say five at a time.*

The Mysteries of the Rosary

*The Joyful Mysteries are said on Mondays and
Saturdays.*
The Mysteries of Light on Thursdays.
The Sorrowful on Tuesdays and Fridays.
The Glorious on Wednesdays and Sundays.

The twenty mysteries are:

The Five Joyful Mysteries

1. The Annunciation
2. The Visitation
3. The Nativity
4. The Presentation in the Temple
5. The Finding of the Child Jesus in the Temple

The Five Mysteries of Light

1. The Baptism in the Jordan
2. The Wedding at Cana
3. The Proclamation of the Kingdom of God
4. The Transfiguration
5. The Institution of the Eucharist

The Five Sorrowful Mysteries

1. The Prayer and Agony in the Garden
2. The Scourging at the Pillar
3. The Crowning with Thorns
4. The Carrying of the Cross
5. The Crucifixion and Death of Our Lord

The Five Glorious Mysteries

1. The Resurrection
2. The Ascension of Christ into Heaven
3. The Descent of the Holy Spirit on the Apostles
4. The Assumption
5. The Coronation of the Blessed Virgin Mary in Heaven
   and the Glory of all the Saints

After the last mystery we say the:

Salve Regina (Hail Holy Queen)

Attributed to several sources; probable author Herman the Lame (1013-1054), a monk of Reichenau

Salve, Regína, mater misericórdiæ; vita, dulcédo, et spes nostra, salve. Ad te clamámus, éxsules fílii Evae. Ad te suspirámus, geméntes et flentes in hac lacrimárum valle. Eia ergo, advocáta nostra, illos tuos misericórdes óculos ad nos convérte. Et Iesum, benedíctum fructum ventris tui, nobis post hoc exsílium osténde. O clemens, O pia, O dulcis Virgo María.

Hail, holy Queen, Mother of Mercy; hail, our life, our sweetness and our hope. To thee do we cry, poor banished children of Eve; to thee do we send up our sighs, mourning and weeping in this valley of tears. Turn then, most gracious advocate, thine eyes of mercy towards us; and after this our exile, show unto us the blessed fruit of thy womb Jesus. O clement, O loving, O sweet Virgin Mary.

V. Ora pro nobis sancta Dei Génetrix.

V. Pray for us O Holy Mother of God.

R. Ut digni efficiamur promissiónibus Christi.

R. That we may be made worthy of the promises of Christ.

Let us pray

O God, whose only-begotten Son, by his life, death and resurrection, has purchased for us the rewards of eternal life; grant we beseech thee, that meditating on these mysteries of the most holy Rosary of the Blessed Virgin Mary, we may both imitate what they contain and obtain what they promise, through the same Christ Our Lord.
R. Amen.

The Angelus

The custom of saying the Angelus at 6 a.m., noon and 6 p.m. goes back to the thirteenth century.

V. Angelus Dómini, nuntiávit Maríae,

V. The angel of the Lord declared unto Mary,

R. Et concépit de Spíritu Sancto.

R. And she conceived of the Holy Spirit.

Ave María...

Hail Mary...

V. Ecce ancilla Domini.

V. Behold the handmaid of the Lord.

R. Fiat mihi secúndum verbum tuum.

R. Be it done to me according to thy word.

Ave María...

Hail Mary...

V. Et Verbum caro factum est,

V. And the word was made flesh,

R. Et habitávit in nobis.

R. And dwelt among us.

Ave María...

Hail Mary...

V. Ora pro nobis, sancta

V. Pray for us O holy

Dei Génetrix,
R. Ut digni efficiámur promissiónibus Christi.

Mother of God,
R. That we may be made worthy of the promises of Christ.

Orémus.
Grátiam tuam, quaésumus, Dómine, méntibus nostris infúnde; ut qui, ángelo nuntiánte, Christi Fílii tui incarnatiónem cognóvimus, per passiónem eius et crucem ✠, ad resurrectiónis glóriam perducámur. Per eúndem Christum Dóminum nostrum.
R. Amen.

Let us pray.
Pour forth, we beseech thee O Lord, thy grace into our hearts that we to whom the incarnation of Christ, thy son, was made known by the message of an angel, may by his passion and cross ✠ be brought to the glory of his resurrection through the same Christ, Our Lord.
R. Amen.

Regina Caeli (by Gregory V)

*A twelfth century Evening Prayer antiphon for the Easter
Season. Since the thirteenth century, it has been used as
the seasonal antiphon in honour of the Blessed Virgin
after Night Prayer. Since 1743 it has replaced the
Angelus in the Easter Season.*

Regína cæli, lætáre. Allelúia.	Queen of heaven, rejoice. Alleluia:
Quia quem meruísti portáre. Allelúia.	For he whom you did merit to bear. Alleluia.
Resurréxit, sicut dixit. Allelúia.	Has risen, as he said. Alleluia.
Ora pro nobis, Deum. Allelúia.	Pray for us to God. Alleluia.
Gaude et lætáre, Virgo María, Allelúia.	Rejoice and be glad, O Virgin Mary. Alleluia.
Quia surréxit Dominus vere. Allelúia.	For the Lord has truly risen. Alleluia.
Orémus.	Let us pray.
Deus, qui per resurrectiónem Fílii tui, Dómini nostri Iesu Christi, mundum lætificáre dignátus es: præsta, quǽsumus; ut, per eius Genitrícem Vírginem Maríam, pérpetuæ capiámus	O God, who gave joy to the world through the resurrection of your Son our Lord Jesus Christ, grant, we beseech you, that through the intercession of the Virgin Mary, his

gáudia vitae. Per eúndem Christum Dóminum nostrum. **R.** Amen.	Mother, we may obtain the joys of everlasting life, though the same Christ our Lord. **R.** Amen.

A Child's Prayer to Mary

From the hymn Memento Rerum Conditur.

Mary, mother whom we bless,
full of grace and tenderness,
defend me from the devil's power
and greet me in my dying hour.

Memorare (Latin version)

Ascribed to St Bernard (1090-1153)

Memoráre, o piíssima Virgo María,
non esse audítum a sǽculo,
quemquam ad tua curréntem præsídia,
tua implorántem auxília, tua peténtem suffrágia esse derelíctum.
Ego tali animátus confidéntia ad te,
Virgo Vírginum, Mater, curro; ad te vénio; coram te gemens peccátor assísto.
Noli, Mater Verbi, verba mea despícere, sed audi propitia et exáudi.
Amen.

Memorare

Remember, O most gracious Virgin Mary,
that never was it known that anyone
who fled to thy protection,
implored thy help, or sought thy intercession, was left
unaided.
Inspired by this confidence I fly unto thee,
O Virgin of virgins, my Mother.
To thee do I come, before thee I stand, sinful and
sorrowful.
O Mother of the Word Incarnate,
despise not my petitions,
but in thy mercy hear and answer me
Amen.

Prayer for England

*In the Middle Ages, England was known as Our Lady's
Dowry, because there were more churches dedicated to
Mary than to any other title.*

*This prayer, in its original form written by Cardinal
Merry del Val, has traditionally been said at Benediction.
It is a prayer for the unity of the Church in England.*

O Blessed Virgin Mary, Mother of God, and our most
gentle queen and mother, look down in mercy upon
England, your dowry, and upon us all who greatly hope
and trust in you. By you it was that Jesus, our Saviour

and our hope, was given to the world; and he has given you to us that we may hope still more.

Plead for us your children, whom you received and accepted at the foot of the cross, O mother of sorrows. Pray for our separated brethren, that in the one true fold of Christ, we may all be united under the care of Pope N., the chief shepherd of Christ's flock. Pray for us all, dear mother, that by faith, and fruitful in good works, we may all deserve to see and praise God, together with you in our heavenly home.

We Fly to Thy Protection

Sub Tuum Praesidium

We fly to thy protection, O holy Mother of God, despise not our petitions in our necessities, but deliver us always from all dangers, O glorious and blessed Virgin.
Amen.

Sub tuum praesidium confugimus, Sancta Dei Genetrix, nostras deprecationes ne despicias in necessitatibus nostris, sed a periculis cunctis libera nos semper, Virgo gloriosa et benedicta.
Amen.

The Church's Oldest Prayer to Our Lady

*Translation of the Greek from which the
prayer Sub Tuum is derived.*

O Mother of God, we take refuge in your loving care. Let not our plea to you pass unheeded in the trials that beset us, but deliver us from danger, for you alone are truly pure, you alone are truly blessed.

Tota Pulchra Es

You are all beautiful, Mary,
and there is no original stain in you.
Tota pulchra es, Maria,
et macula originalis non est in te.

Totus Tuus

St Louis-Marie Grignon de Montfort (1673-1716)
Totus tuus ego sum, et omnia mea tua sunt,
O Virgo, super omnia benedicta.
I am all yours, and all that is mine is yours,
O Virgin, blessed above all.

Maria, Mater Gratiae

Mary, Mother of grace, Mother of mercy,
protect me from the enemy and receive me at the hour of death.
Maria, Mater gratiae, Mater misericordiae,
tu me ab hoste protege et mortis hora suscipe.

Sancta Maria, Succurre Miseris

Holy Mary, hasten to the aid of the afflicted,.
support the fainthearted, comfort the sorrowful,
pray for your people, intercede on behalf of the clergy,
intercede for devout women;
may all who celebrate your holy memory come to know
your assistance.

Sancta Maria, succurre miseris, iuva pusillanimes,
refove flebiles, ora pro populo,
interveni pro clero, intercede pro devoto femineo sexu:
sentiant omnes tuum iuvamen, quiccumque celebrant
tuam sanctam commemorationem.

IN SICKNESS AND DEATH

Prayer for a Happy Death

From the Roman Missal

Father, you made us in your own image and your Son
accepted death for our salvation.

Help us to keep watch in prayer at all times.

May we be free from sin when we leave this world and
rejoice in peace with you for ever.

Prayer for the Sick

From the Roman Missal

Father, your Son accepted our sufferings
to teach us the virtue of patience in human illness.

Hear the prayers we offer for our sick brothers and sisters.

May all who suffer pain, illness or disease realise that
they are chosen to be saints and know that they are joined
to Christ in his suffering for the salvation of the world.

Prayer for the Dying

From the Roman Missal

God of power and mercy, you have made death itself
the gateway to eternal life.

Look with love on our dying brother (sister) and make
him (her) one with your Son in his suffering and death,

that, sealed with the blood of Christ,
he (she) may come before you free from sin.

Prayer for the Dead

This is the traditional Introit from the Mass for the Dead
Eternal rest grant unto them, O Lord
and let perpetual light shine upon them.

Prayer Immediately after Death

Immediately after death has occurred, all may kneel
while one of those present leads the following prayer:
Saints of God, come to his/her aid!
Come to meet him/her, angels of the Lord!
R. Receive him/her, angels of the Lord!
May Christ, who called you, take you to himself;
may angels lead you to Abraham's side. **R.**
Give him/her eternal rest, O Lord, and may your light
shine on him/her for ever. **R.**
The following prayer is added:
Let us pray.
All powerful and merciful God, we commend to you N.,
your servant. In your mercy and love,
blot out the sins he/she has committed through human
weakness.
In this world he/she died: let him/her live with you for
ever.
We ask this through Christ our Lord. **R.** Amen.

EXPOSITION AND BENEDICTION

Rite of Exposition and Benediction

Toward the beginning of the thirteenth century, great emphasis was being placed on the truth of the Real Presence of Christ in the Blessed Sacrament. Although Catholics had always believed that Jesus is actually present in the Eucharist, the fact was now being stressed to counteract some false ideas that were prevalent at the time. To correct mistaken notions and even superstition in regard to the doctrine, the Church fostered a renewal in the faith and devotion toward the Real Presence. In 1246, the feast of Corpus Christi, honouring the Body of Our Lord, was established. Also in this period, St Thomas Aquinas, the 'Angelic Doctor,' composed his beautiful hymns praising the Holy Eucharist. (Anthony Teolis, "Mary at Benediction", *Homiletic and Pastoral Review*, vol. XCVII, no. 2, p. 54.)

Exposition

After the people have assembled, a song may be sung while the minister comes to the altar. If the holy Eucharist is not reserved at the altar where the exposition is to take place, the minister puts on a humeral veil and brings the sacrament from the place of reservation; he is accompanied by servers or by the faithful with lighted candles.

The ciborium or monstrance should be placed upon the table of the altar, which is covered with a cloth. After exposition, if the monstrance is used, the minister incenses the sacrament. If the adoration is to be lengthy, he may then withdraw.

Adoration

During the exposition there should be prayers, songs and readings to direct the attention of the faithful to the worship of Christ the Lord.

To encourage a prayerful spirit, there should be readings from Scripture with a homily or brief exhortation to develop a better understanding of the eucharistic mystery. It is desirable also for the people to respond to the word of God by singing and to spend some periods of time in religious silence.

Part of the Liturgy of the Hours, especially the principal hours, may be celebrated before the Blessed Sacrament when there is a lengthy period of exposition. This liturgy extends the praise and thanksgiving offered to God in the eucharistic celebration to the several hours of the day; it directs the prayers of the Church to Christ and through him to the Father in the name of the whole world. One of the following hymns may be sung:

O salutáris Hóstia
Quæ cæli pandis óstium.

O Saving Victim opening
wide The gates of heav'n
to man below!

Bella premunt hostília;
Da robur fer auxílium.

Our foes press on from
every side; Thine aid
supply, Thy strength
bestow.

Uni trinóque Dómino
Sit sempitérna glória:

To Thy great name be
endless praise Immortal
Godhead, One in Three;

Qui vitam sine término,
Nobis donet in pátria.

Oh, grant us endless length
of days, In our true native
land with Thee.

Amen.

Amen.

or: Adoro Te Devote (page 37-39)

Benediction

Eucharistic hymn and incensation

Toward the end, the priest or deacon goes to the altar,
genuflects and kneels. As a hymn or other Eucharistic
song is sung, the minister, while kneeling, incenses the
rament, if the exposition has taken place with the
monstrance. A hymn such as the following may be sung:

Tantum ergo Sacraméntum
Venerémur cérnui:

Therefore we, before him
bending,
This great Sacrament revere;

Et antíquum documéntum

Types and shadows have their ending

Novo cedat rítui:

for the newer rite is here;

Præstet fides suppleméntum

Faith, our outward sense befriending,

Sénsuum deféctui.

Makes the inward vision clear.

Genitóri, Genitóque

Glory let us give, and blessing

Laus et jubilátio.

To the Father and the Son;

Salus, honor, virtus quoque

Honour, might and praise addressing,

Sit et benedíctio;

While eternal ages run;

Procedénti ab utróque;

Ever to his love confessing,

Compar sit laudátio.

Who, from both, with both is one.

Amen.

Amen.

V. Panem de cælo præstítisti eis (T.P. Allelúia).

V. You have given them bread from heaven. (Easter time: Alleluia).

R. Omne delectaméntum in se habéntem (T.P. Alleluia).

R. Having all sweetness within it. (Easter Time: Alleluia).

Oremus.

Let us pray.

Deus, qui nobis sub sacraménto mirábili, passiónis tuæ memóriam

Lord Jesus Christ, you gave us the Eucharist as the memorial of your reliquísti: tríbue, quǽsumus, ita nos córporis et Sánguinis tui sacra mystéria venerári, ut redemptiónis tuæ fructum in nobis iúgiter sentiámus: Qui vivis et regnas in sǽcula sæculórum.

R. Amen.

suffering and death. May our worship of this sacrament of your body and blood help us to experience the salvation you won for us and the peace of the kingdom where you live with the Father and the Holy Spirit, one God, for ever and ever.

R. Amen.

Then the priest or deacon makes the Sign of the Cross over the people with the monstrance or ciborium, in silence.

The Divine Praises

Blessed be God.

Blessed be his holy Name.

Blessed be Jesus Christ, true God and true Man.

Blessed be the name of Jesus.

Blessed be his most Sacred Heart.

Blessed be his most Precious Blood.

Blessed be Jesus in the most holy Sacrament of the Altar.

Blessed be the Holy Spirit, the Paraclete.

Blessed be the great Mother of God, Mary, most holy.

Blessed be her holy and Immaculate Conception.

Blessed be her glorious Assumption.

Blessed be the name of Mary, Virgin and Mother.

Blessed be St Joseph, her spouse most chaste.

Blessed be God in his Angels and in his Saints.

EVENING PRAYER

An order for Evening Prayer

V. O God, come to our aid.
R. O Lord, make haste to help us.
Glory be to the Father, and to the Son, and to the Holy
Spirit, as it was in the beginning, is now and ever shall
be, world without end. Amen. (Alleluia)

(A suitable hymn such as the following is said)
O Trinity of blessed light,
O Unity of princely might,
The fiery sun now goes his way;
Shed thou within our hearts thy ray.

To thee our morning song of praise,
To thee our evening prayer we raise;
Thy glory suppliant we adore
For ever and for evermore.

All laud to God the Father be;
All praise, eternal Son, to thee;
All glory, as is ever meet,
To God the Holy Paraclete. Amen.

One or more of the following psalms can be said:

Psalm 110

The Lord's revelation to my Master;
'Sit on my right;
your foes I will put beneath your feet'.

The Lord will wield from Sion
your sceptre of power;
rule in the midst of all your foes.

A prince from the day of your birth
on the holy mountains;
from the womb before the dawn I begot you.

The Lord has sworn an oath he will not change.
'You are a priest for ever,
a priest like Melchizedek of old.'

The Master standing at your right hand
will shatter kings in the day of his wrath.

He shall drink from the stream by the wayside
and therefore he shall lift up his head.

Glory be to the Father, and to the Son, and to the Holy
Spirit, as it...

Psalm 16

Preserve me, God, I take refuge in you.
I say to the Lord: 'You are my God.
My happiness lies in you alone'.

He has put into my heart a marvellous love
for the faithful ones who dwell in his land.
Those who choose other gods increase their sorrows.
Never will I offer their offerings of blood.
Never will I take their name upon my lips.

O Lord, it is you who are my portion and cup;
it is you yourself who are my prize.
The lot marked out for me is my delight:
welcome indeed the heritage that falls to me!

I will bless the Lord who gives me counsel,
who even at night directs my heart.
I keep the Lord ever in my sight:
since he is at my right hand, I shall stand firm.

And so my heart rejoices, my soul is glad;
even my body shall rest in safety.
For you will not leave my soul among the dead,
nor let your beloved know decay.

You will show me the path of life,
the fullness of joy in your presence,
at your right hand happiness for ever.

Glory be to the Father, and to the Son, and to the Holy
Spirit, as it...

*(Other Psalms suitable for Evening prayer include
Psalms 72, 111, 126 & 127)*

Scripture Reading 2 Cor 1:3-4

Let us give thanks to the God and Father of our Lord
Jesus Christ, the merciful Father, the God from whom all
help comes! He helps us in all our troubles, so that we are
able to help those who have all kinds of troubles, using
the same help that we ourselves have received from God.

Magnificat (Canticle of Mary)

My soul glorifies the Lord,
my spirit rejoices in God, my Saviour.
He looks on his servant in her lowliness;
henceforth all ages will call me blessed.

The Almighty works marvels for me.
Holy his name!
His mercy is from age to age,
on those who fear him.
He puts forth his arm in strength and

scatters the proud-hearted.
He casts the mighty from their thrones
and raises the lowly.

He fills the starving with good things,
sends the rich away empty.

He protects Israel, his servant,
remembering his mercy,
the mercy promised to our fathers,
to Abraham and his sons for ever.

Glory be to the Father, and to the Son, and to the Holy
Spirit, as it...

Short Responsory

R. How manifold are your works, O Lord. *(Repeat)*
V. In wisdom you have made them all.
R. How manifold are your works, O Lord.
V. Glory be to the Father, and to the Son, and to the
Holy Spirit.
R. How manifold are your works, O Lord.

Intercessions

V. May your kingdom of peace and justice be realised on
earth as in heaven.
R. Lord, hear our prayer.
V. Show yourself to all who seek you in sincerity of heart.

R. Lord, hear our prayer.

V. O Lord Jesus Christ, light of all the nations, shine upon all those who walk in darkness and in the shadow of death.

R. Lord, hear our prayer.

V. Be with all those who suffer in body, mind or spirit.

R. Lord, hear our prayer.

V. Show your mercy to the dead, bring them to rejoice in the company of the Blessed Virgin Mary and all your saints.

R. Lord, hear our prayer.

Our Father...

Concluding Prayer

Let our evening prayer rise before you like incense, Lord,
and may your blessing shower down upon us:
so that now and forever your grace may heal and save us.
We ask this through our Lord Jesus Christ your Son,
who lives and reigns in the unity of the Holy Spirit,
ever one God, world without end. Amen.

✠ May the Lord bless us, keep us from all evil and bring us to everlasting life. Amen.

Night Prayer

V. O God, come to our aid
R. O Lord, make haste to help us.
Glory be to the Father, and to the Son, and to the Holy
Spirit, as it was in the beginning, is now and ever shall
be, world without end.
Amen. (Alleluia)

(The following or a suitable hymn is said)
Before we end our day, O Lord,
We make this prayer to you:
That you continue in your love
To guard your people here.

Give us this night untroubled rest
And build our strength anew:
Your Splendour driving far away
All darkness of the foe.

All glory be to you, O Christ
Who saved mankind from death
To share with you the Father's love
And in the Spirit live.

One or both of the following psalms may be said:

Psalm 4

When I call, answer me,
O God of justice;
from anguish you released me,
have mercy and hear me!

How long, you people,
will your hearts be closed,
will you love what is futile
and seek what is false?

It is the Lord who grants favours
to those whom he loves;
the Lord hears me
whenever I call him.

Fear him: do not sin:
ponder on your bed and be still.
Make justice your sacrifice
and trust in the Lord.

'What can bring us happiness?' many say.
Let the light of your face shine on us, O Lord.

You have put into my heart a greater joy than they have
from abundance of corn and new wine.

I will lie down in peace
and sleep comes at once
for you alone,
Lord, make me dwell in safety.

Glory be to the Father, and to the Son, and to the Holy
Spirit, as it...

Psalm 133

O come, bless the Lord,
all you who serve the Lord,
who stand in the house of the Lord,
in the courts of the house of our God.

Lift up your hands to the holy place
And bless the Lord through the night.
May the Lord bless you from Sion,
He who made both heaven and earth.

Glory be to the Father, and to the Son, and to the Holy
Spirit, as it...

Scripture Reading (1 P 5:8-9)

Be calm but vigilant, because your enemy the devil is
prowling round like a roaring lion, looking for someone
to devour. Stand up to him, strong in faith.

Short Responsory

R. Into your hands, Lord, I commend my spirit. *(Repeat)*
V. You have redeemed us, Lord God of truth.
R. Into your hands, Lord, I commend my spirit.
V. Glory be to the Father, and to the Son and to the Holy Spirit.
R. Into your hands, Lord, I commend my spirit.

Nunc Dimittis (Canticle of Simeon)

Ant. Save us, Lord while we are awake; protect us while we are asleep; that we may keep watch with Christ and rest with him in peace (Alleluia).

Now, Lord, you have kept your word:
let your servant go in peace.

With my own eyes I have seen the salvation
which you have prepared in the sight of every people:

A light to reveal you to the nations
and the glory of your people Israel.

Glory be to the Father, and to the Son, and to the Holy Spirit, as it...

Ant. Save us, Lord while we are awake; protect us while we are asleep; That we may keep watch with Christ and rest with him in peace (Alleluia).

Concluding Prayer

Lighten our darkness we beseech you O Lord, and by your great mercy defend us from all the perils and dangers of this night; for the love of your only Son, our Saviour Jesus Christ. Amen.

Blessing

✠ May the Lord grant us a quiet night and a perfect end. Amen. May the souls of the faithful departed, through the mercy of God, rest in peace. Amen.

An anthem to the Blessed Virgin Mary is now said. During Ordinary Time the **Salve Regina** *(page 52). During Eastertide, the* **Regina Cæli** *(page 55).*

Informative Catholic Reading

We hope that you have enjoyed reading this booklet.

If you would like to find out more about CTS booklets - we'll send you our free information pack and catalogue.

Please send us your details:

Name ....

Address ....

....

....

Postcode ....

Telephone...

Email ....

Send to: CTS, 40-46 Harleyford Road,
            Vauxhall, London
            SE11 5AY

Tel: 020 7640 0042
Fax: 020 7640 0046
Email: info@cts-online.org.uk